OPTIONS TRADING STRATEGIES

A COMPLETE GUIDE ON HOW TO MAKE HIGH PROFITS WITH PROVEN STRATEGIES IN OPTIONS TRADING, INCLUDING A BEST DAY AND SWING TRADING STRATEGIES

ROBERT EATON

COPYRIGHT

CONTENTS

INTRODUCTION

Options can be a bit hard to get your head around at first since so many of us are used to looking at the market as a thing that goes up or down. Options bring a sideways and a different vertical element to it via spreads and volatility estimates. More advanced options strategies take full advantage of volatility and are more math-focused, so if this interests you, you should go for them.

You can choose to borrow, of course, but you need to do this only if it is in line with your risk management math. Risk management is what will make or break your results and at the center of quantitative risk management is your risk per trade. Keep this consistent and line up your success rate and reward to risk ratios, and you'll make money as a mathematical certainty.

Generally, a good options trade can expect around 50-80% returns on their capital. As you grow in size, this return amount will decrease naturally. However, to start off with, these are beyond excellent returns.

Always make sure you're well-capitalized since this is the downfall of many traders. You need to be patient with the process. A lot of people rush headfirst into the market without adequate capitalization or learning and soon find that the markets are far tougher than they thought. So, always ensure the mental stress you place yourself in is low and that you're never in a position where you 'have' to make money trading.

Make sure you take the time to understand all the concepts covered in this book and then actually implement them in real life. If you don't put this knowledge you've gained into practice, you will forget it, and it would've all been just a waste of time. Remember to be patient, manage your risk, and keep learning more as you gain experience in the market. That's what makes a good trader

The learning curve might get steep at times, but given the rewards on offer, this is a small price to pay. Keep hammering away at your skills, and soon you'll find yourself trading options profitably, and everything will be worth it. How much can you expect to make trading options?

CHAPTER 1: OPTIONS TRADING OVERVIEW

What is Options Trading?

Option contracts usually refer to the purchase or sale of certain assets.

An option is a contract between two parties (a buyer and a seller), in which whoever buys the option acquires the right to exercise what the agreement indicates, although he will not have an obligation to do so.

Option contracts commonly refer to purchasing or selling certain assets, stocks, stock indices, bonds, or others. These contracts establish that the operation must be carried out on a pre-established date (European, since the US exercise at any time) at a fixed price when the contract after signing the contract. Purchasing an option to buy or sell is necessary to make an initial disbursement (called "premium"). Purchasing an opportunity to buy or sell is essential to make an initial disbursement known as premium.

Premium value depends fundamentally on the asset's price as the contract's object has on the market. The variability of that price and the period between the contract signing date and expiration

Call and Put

The options that grant the right to buy are called 'Call,' and those that allow the right to sell is called 'Put.' Additionally, it is called European options that can only be exercised on the date of exercise and American Options that can be used during the contract's life.

When the time comes for the buying party to exercise the option, if it does, two situations occur:

Whoever appears as the seller of the option will be obliged to do what they said contract indicates; that is, sell or buy the asset to the counterparty, in case it decides to exercise its right to buy or sell.

Who appears as the option buyer will have the right to buy or sell the asset? However, if it doesn't suit you, you can refrain from making the transaction.

An option contract usually contains the following specifications:

- Exercise date: the expiration date of the right is included in the option.
- Exercise price: agreed price for the asset's purchase/sale referred to in the contract (called an underlying asset).
- Option premium or price: amount paid to the counterparty to acquire the right to buy or sell.
- Rights acquired with the purchase of an option: Call (right of purchase) and Put (right of sale).
- Types of Option: there may be Europeans, are exercised on the date of exercise or American, used at any time during the contract. There are, besides, other more complex types of options, the so-called "Exotic Options."

In international financial markets, the types of options traded on organized exchanges are typically American and European. For example, in Chile, as with futures, there is no stock market for opportunities.

Practical Example

Purchase of a call option by an importing company to secure the Euro price on that day.

To better understand the use of options, this example is presented by an importing company that wants to ensure against increases in the Euro price.

To do so, you can buy a European call option today that gives you the right to buy a million euros, within three months, at $550 per euro. To acquire that right, the company pays $2 per euro; that is, the option premium has a cost of $2,000,000.

If on the expiration date of the option, the price of the euro in the market is over $550 (for example, at $560), the company will exercise the opportunity to buy them, as it will only pay $550 per euro.

On the contrary, if on that date the market price of the Euro was below $550 (for example at $530), it means the company will not exercise the option, since it makes no sense to pay $550 per euro on purchase at the market at $530; In this case, the option expires without being exercised.

The cash flows are as follows:

Today (April 10, 20XX).

Buy a European call option, which gives you the right to buy USD 1,000,000 to $550 on October 10, 20XX, as the value of the premium is 2 and 1,000,000 contracts are purchased (which means that the notional of the agreement is the US $1) there is a cash outlay of $2,000,000 for that concept.

Expiration date (October 30, 20XX).

If the Euro is above the option's exercise price, it is exercised, and $550 per euro is paid, $550,000,000.

Otherwise, the option expires if used, and the euros are acquired in the market.

3

The euros purchased are used to cancel the importation of goods or services:

The following table shows the results of the operation:

Suppose the option contract's expiration date and the market exchange rate is lower than the call option's exercise price. The importer ends up paying the market price per euro, the premium cost (in strict rigor, the bonus' value is updated for the interest that is earned if, instead of paying compensation price, that money was deposited).

Otherwise, One Euro will cost equal to the exercise price plus the premium. That is, the importer will have made sure to pay a maximum of $552 per euro.

Notes:

On the expiration date, if the Euro is lower than the exercise price, the value of the call option will be zero (as it is not appropriate to exercise the purchase right), whereas, if the opposite occurs, the value of the call option will correspond to the difference between those two prices.

That result represents how much money was paid or saved by the fact of coverage.

Currencies are acquired when it is not optimal to exercise the option or exercise the right of purchase when exercising that right is an optimal decision.

Finally, note that if a forward-type contract with the same delivery price were used to perform the same coverage, the importer would have ended up always paying $550. However, it would not have had the opportunities (which may appear when hedging with call options) to benefit from declines in the market exchange rate.

Note that the operation is performed more comfortably. When purchasing, you pay a premium option and, on the expiration, at least the agreed price.

CHAPTER 2: OPTIONS TRADING STRATEGIES: THE BASICS

Strategies are simply the tools that you employ to maximize your return on investment and reduce your risk exposure. In essence, options trading strategies help you to trade successfully. In options trading, there is much more to it than just forecasting the movement of a particular underlying asset then making a trade. There are plenty of other ways to make a profit, and this is where any trader who wants to be successful in options trading needs to have a range of strategies at their disposal.

While there is a wide range of strategies that traders can use, it is important to understand that most strategies are not a one-size-fits-all solution. The appropriate strategy for a particular trade will depend on a variety of factors. This means that you may very well have knowledge about a wide range of trading strategies, but unless you can figure out when and how to use them, they may not do you much good.

Bearish Strategies

A bear market means that the same market has a downward trend over a given period of time. When we talk about bearish strategies, it means that the investor believes that the price of an asset will have a downward trend, and therefore, he can build his strategy based on this.

The main advantage of using bearish strategies is that they are very flexible. Bearish strategies enable you to profit when the underlying asset decreases in price while giving you some level of control over your risk exposure. There are different types of bearish strategies, and these include:

Bullish Strategies

A bear market means that the same market has an upward trend over a given period of time. Contrary to bearish strategies, bullish strategies are adopted by the investor who believes that the price of an asset will have an upward trend and will base his entire strategy on this intuition.

Bullish strategies are used when you expect the price of the underlying asset to increase. For instance, if the current price of a stock is $100, and you predict that in a month, it will rise to $110 or any other figure, then, in this case, bullish strategies will be the appropriate strategies to use.

Neutral Strategies

When the investor believes that the market will have neither upward nor downward trends, then he will adopt strategies said neutral that will be based on that intuition.

Picking the Right Trading Strategy

Even the most seasoned traders will sometimes have trouble deciding which strategy is best for a particular trade. This means that while choosing a strategy, do not be overly concerned about the best strategy but rather finding one that is suitable for your goal or objective.

Here are the main considerations to keep in mind when selecting the right strategy.

Consider your Outlook

Do you expect the price of the underlying security to rise or fall? If you are expecting the price to rise, then bullish strategies are more appropriate for that particular trade. When you expect the price of the underlying stock to fall, bearish strategies may be the more appropriate option. Whatever your outlook or prediction is, use that as a guide to help you choose the appropriate strategy for the position or trade you want to enter.

Weigh the Risk vs. Reward

Each strategy carries a different risk/reward ratio. Picking the right strategy will require you to weigh how much you stand to lose vs. how much you stand to gain. Any trade that you make should be guided by the ratio of risk to reward. Risk management is an integral part of successful options trading so, the risk/reward ratio should play a big role in not just the kind of trades you pick but also the strategies that you choose to employ.

Some strategies such as vertical spreads are commonly used in situations where you want to lower the cost of the trade but still retain the profit potential. Such strategies are great risk management tools. It is important to understand which strategies are effective in minimizing your risk exposure because, ultimately, your goal in trading is to make profit, not losses.

Trading Level

Your broker will typically assign you a trading level. This level will determine the kind of strategies that you can use while trading. If you have been assigned a low trading level, the range of trading strategies you can use will be limited because trading strategies with higher risk levels typically require a higher trading level. This means that you

7

need to understand the level of risk allowance that is appropriate for your trading level.

Complexity

It is best to keep it simple, especially if you are just starting out. Go for strategies that you have a thorough understanding of because you will understand when, where, and how to use them. When you use a complicated strategy, you may have a harder time figuring out the potential profits or risks of a particular trade, and this can cause you to pick the wrong trades.

Simpler strategies are also easier to use when trying to determine the best entry and exit points of a trade. You can always move on to the complex strategies once you have gained a better understanding of them, but more often than not, you will find that the best strategy is the one that you understand well.

CHAPTER 3: THE 4 BASICS STRATEGIES. BUYING AND SELLING OPTIONS

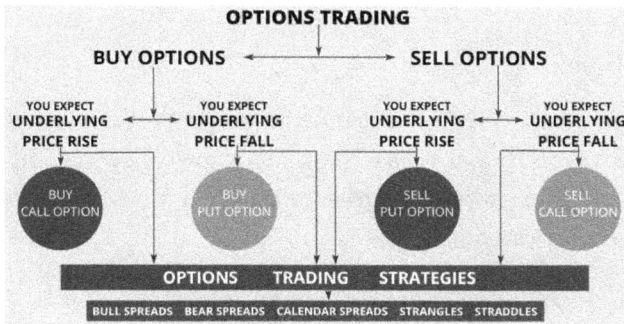

Long Call

This strategy is best used when you are expecting a significant rise in the price of the underlying security. This strategy is pretty simple and simply involves using the buy to open order to purchase calls on the asset that you expect to increase in price. If you are expecting the rise in price to be swift, then buy a contract with a short expiration. On the other hand, if you predict a slower rise in the price of the underlying asset, a long-term contract will be more appropriate.

Pros:

- A simple and straightforward strategy
- Ideal for beginners
- It can be used by people with a low trading level
- It does not require a lot of capital
- Offers leverage that makes it possible to make a lot of profit with a small investment.
- You can easily make further transactions and convert the strategy into a different one

Cons:

- You have no protection if the underlying stock price falls in value
- The value of calls decreases with time, so your trade is susceptible to the effects of time decay

Short Call

This option strategy is a bearish strategy generally adopted when a trader is expecting a decrease in a stock price, so he sells the call option. Same thing when the price of the stock doesn't increase above the call's strike price before the expiration.

Long Put

A long put is a simple strategy that you can use when you are expecting the price of an asset to decrease in value. It involves a single transaction, buying puts. In this instance, you buy puts expecting the underlying assets to go down in price and profit from the difference between the strike price and the market price.

Long puts are ideal as both bearish and bullish trading strategies because they offer leverage. This means that you stand to potentially make big returns on investments without necessarily investing huge amounts.

Pros:

- Huge potential profits and limited losses
- Ideal for beginners since it is simple and straight forward
- Low commissions charged

Cons:

- Huge potential losses if the underlying asset increases in value
- The value of your contract decreases with time due to time decay

Short Put

When you are expecting a downturn in the price of an underlying security, you can use a short put strategy. This involves a single transaction where you sell or write contracts. In this case, you make a profit when the price of the underlying asset drops. Since the profit potential on short puts is limited, it is ideal for when you expect only a marginal drop in the price of the underlying asset.

When you use a short-put trading strategy, you are effectively establishing a credit position since you get your profits upfront.

Pros:

- You get your profit upfront
- Requires a single transaction, so commission fees are low

Cons:

- Potential for big losses
- The profit potential is limited
- Requires high trading level

CHAPTER 4: LEAPS IN OPTIONS TRADING

Trading with LEAPS

The acronym LEAPS stands for Long-term Equity Anticipation Securities. They are a type of option with expiration dates that are longer than normal. They last for at least 1 year and sometimes go as far as 3 years into the future. As mentioned earlier, the expiration dates of options are typically a few months into the future. The typical option expiration ranges are 3 months, 6 months, and 9 months.

This is because options are typically a short-term way of investing.

LEAPS step away from the norm and have a longer shelf-life compared to your average option. They still possess the qualities as a normal option. It appeals to investors that want a long-term invest-ment without being obliged by that investment. It also appeals to the investor who is anticipating a profitable yield from a particular market in the future but does not have the capital at hand to make that substantial investment. They are more affordable than such assets like stock because, despite the long expiration date, they are still options and thus, stick to option price ranges. It normally has a slightly higher price than other short-term contracts

LEAPS have a seat at the options table because sometimes the value of the associated asset needs more time to appreciate. Typical options expire in a few months. These options can yield profits in a short amount of time, but there is also the risk that the transaction might not be as profitable if the stock or other associated asset does not move significantly up or down.

They are the solution that allows the time for appreciation of the associated asset. A trader can even extend the expiration on that LEAP option with another LEAP if the time period is still too short for the asset to reach profitability. For example, a LEAP with an expiration date of 2 years can be held for 1 year then be sold to replace with a 3-year expiration date. This is called rolled LEAPS.

Rolling the option forward is normally relatively inexpensive because it still carries the same characteristics. Other factors can become unpredictable, though. Such factors include interest rates, dividends, and volatility.

The question that stumps many traders about LEAPS is whether to use a call option or a put option. The answer to that is dependent on whether the trader expects a bullish or bearish price movement. If the trader believes that the associated asset is bullish by the expiration date, he or she should buy call options. If instead, he or she believes that the associated asset will drop in value by the expiration date, then the trader should buy put options.

Best Strategies for Using LEAPS

Some strategies work best when it pertains to LEAPS, and this list includes:

- Long call: This involves the purchase of LEAPS call options in anticipation of a long-term bullish trend in the market.
- Long put: This involves the purchase of LEAPS put options in anticipation of a long-term bearish trend in the market.
- Rolling LEAPS options: As mentioned earlier, this involves

selling the LEAPS before the expiration date while buying LEAPS with similar characteristics with at least 2-year expiration dates at the same time.

- Bull call spread: This options strategy is considered to reduce the initial cost of buying a call option. This can help offset the higher cost of LEAPS compared to standard options. Only use this strategy if you are confident that there will be a moderate rise in the price of the stock to send it up to the strike price.
- Bull call spread: This is another strategy meant to offset the higher cost of LEAPs. It is a bearish strategy. Profits are earned when the stock prices fall.
- Calendar call spread: This strategy is meant for a trader who wishes to benefit from the associated assets staying stagnant in the market while also benefiting from the long-term call position if the stock becomes more valuable in the future.

Benefits of LEAPS

LEAPS have several benefits, and they include:

They are sustainable as they allow a trader to piggyback off-market trends. This allows the trader to observe the movement of stock prices and have an option to buy or sell without making the full commitment of ownership.

They are less volatile, and so offer greater security. A trader who enters into such an option is looking at a stock that is increasing or decreasing in price over the long haul. This allows the trader the time to really ponder on the profitability of pursuing the asset. This person can use data offered over that time, such as the current trends, news, and terms, to base their future decision.

They can serve great security in your financial portfolio as well as provide shareholders with a greater grip of the stock.

LEAPS allow time for improvisation because the expiration date is longer.

Buying them is cheaper than buying several standard options back to back.

Disadvantages of LEAPS

There are two sides to every coin. So, just as LEAPS are beneficial, there are also a few downsides. The first disadvantage is the strike price. Because they are priced higher, the trader needs to see movement in the asset price to gain a profit, in addition to it taking longer for the option holder to break even.

The longer expiration dates on LEAPS make them less predictable. Therefore, pricing correctly so that a return is seen without the transaction being too costly is made can be difficult. Lastly, the trader will not benefit from any attached dividends or stock repurchases.

They are also sensitive to implied volatility, and so can lower in value when implied volatility drops.

Tips for Getting the Most Out of LEAPS

Pretend as if you are investing. This allows you to search for assets that you are interested in and maybe already have some know-how about. This makes it a lot easier to keep up-to-date with market trends compared to if you do not know anything about the asset and are not interested in learning more.

Make use of the long expiration date. The benefits of the long expiration date have been stated, so ensure that these work to your benefit.

- Choose LEAPS that are more liquid.
- Prepare for the fact that they are more volatile than stocks but less volatile than standard options.
- Set targets for the stock prices in comparison to your LEAPS.

    Knowing those targets will allow the trader to sell at the most profitable time.

- Have an exit strategy in case the option is not working out according to plan.

Always be aware of your position and be prepared to leverage it. Even though the expiration date is far off, you need to keep abreast as to whether the market is playing out as you anticipated. You need to be aware of the fluctuations in the asset's price. This will allow you to decide what makes this transaction the most profitable it can be for you. You can implement strategies like rolling the option forward and selling the first option as a loss so that you can move to another strike price that benefits you more.

CHAPTER 5: VERTICAL SPREAD OPTIONS STRATEGIES

Spread strategies are more advanced in that you don't need to establish a long position. Thus, the cost of establishing a position is a lot lower than with the covered call or the collar trade. While your long-term options trading base should be rooted in those strategies, pursuing spread trades will give you healthy returns in the short term.

Spread trades work very much in principle like collar trades (explained in the following paragraphs), except you will be buying and selling calls (or puts) of the same month and the same type of option in every trade. In other words, while you were selling calls and buying puts with the collar, in this case, you will be buying and selling calls or buying and selling puts.

Vertical Spreads

When it comes to spread trading, there are two categories all types of trades fit into. These are vertical spreads and horizontal spreads. The names sound fancy, but understanding how they work really isn't anywhere near as complicated.

Having said that, these types of trades do crank the complexity level up a bit. If the collar took things up a notch from covered calls, then spread trades do the same with the collar. As beneficial as collars and covered calls are, there is one major disadvantage that those strategies pose to the trader.

They require a long stock purchase. In the case of a covered call, this is an investment, while in the case of a collar, it can be speculative or an investment. Whatever the designation there's no escaping the fact that long stock investment requires a lot of money. What if you wish to emulate Thales' example and get in on low capital values?

This is what the spread strategies address. Options give us the flexibility to play around with the way price moves, and as you'll see, spread trades encompass taking advantage of a wide variety of market behavior.

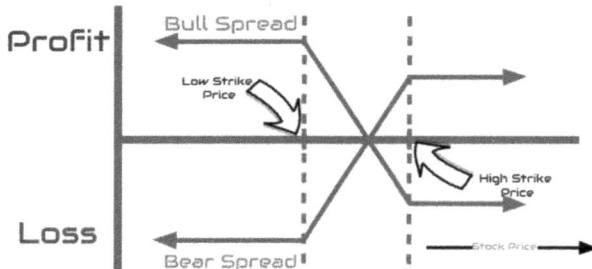

Debit Spreads Options Strategy

A debit spread is created when you purchase two options contracts based on the same underlying asset at different strike rates. The cost of purchasing the option is usually higher than the premium you get for selling. This means that you incur a cost when you open the trade.

Debit spreads work by reducing your investment or cost and, in effect, minimizing your risk exposure. Depending on whether you expect the market price to increase or fall, you can use either a debit call spread or a debit put spread, respectively.

Two of the four Vertical Spreads strategies are the Bull Call spreads and the Bear Put spread because you have to pay a premium when you enter the trade

Bull Call Spreads

One of the biggest benefits of trading options is that you don't need to be terribly worried about the current market situation since your trades are designed to profit in all markets. At the very least, you will have a strategy, no matter what the market is doing. The bull call spread, also called the long call spread, is a strategy for a moderate to a strong bullish market.

In this scenario, you're quite certain that the stock is going to increase in value over the medium term, but you're a bit uncertain about the volatility it is showing. You see, there is a dose of uncertainty with every directional position, and you are compensated for this with higher rewards. Options strategies take this uncertainty away but cap your maximum reward.

Thus, if you're extremely certain that a stock is going to go upwards for sure, buying a long call is probably the best strategy. After all, if you know a stock is going to increase in value, why would you place a cap on your profits by writing a call at a higher strike price?

Such situations are extremely rare; however, and this is where the bull call spread comes into action.

How it Works

With the bull call spread, you will be buying a long call that is either in the money or close to the money and offsetting this price by writing an out-of-the-money call. If the stock goes past the higher strike price, your long call is in profit, but your overall profit is capped to the level of the higher strike price.

If the stock goes below your long call, you have the premium of the higher strike price call to offset your loss, which is simply the premium you paid for the long call. Remember, you're not buying any stock in this strategy, so there is no loss on the stock itself.

Let's continue to use AAPL as an example of this. As of this writing, AAPL is trading at $173.3. The closest at the money call option in the near month is the $170 and $175, which is trading at $6.95 and $4.10, respectively. Now, you could choose either of these strike prices. Remember, you're moderately bullish on the stock but are not sure how high it will go. Given these conditions, let's purchase the 175 call for $4.10.

Now, we need to find a suitable strike price to write a call at. This is a tricky balancing act. Write a call too far away, and you won't receive enough of a premium. Write one too close, and you're not giving your trade enough breathing room. This is why it's essential to keep your time horizon on this trade as short as you can afford to. Ideally, your options will have some time value left on them but not too much time so as to bring price uncertainty into them.

The time decay is evident in the current month's option prices. The $190 option is selling for $0.37, which is a pittance, really. However, let's stick with the current month for now. So, what do our risk and reward look like?

Maximum risk = Premium paid for long call - Premium received for short call = 4.1 -0.37 = 3.73.

Maximum reward = Strike price of short call - Strike price of long call - cost paid for entering the trade = 190-175 - 3.73 = 11.27

Thus, our reward/risk on this 3X. Just to clarify, the prices quoted for an option contract are on a per-share basis. Since every contract contains a hundred shares, you should multiply the price by a hundred to get the full price of the contract.

So, to enter this position, or to purchase a single contract, we will need to spend $373, and if the price hits our higher strike price of $190 then we'll clear $1127 on the trade. These numbers are with the near-month options, of course. Let's look at how the numbers change by taking the far month into consideration.

•Price of far month $175 call= $6.30

•Price of far month $190 call= $0.92

•Cost of entering the trade and maximum risk/share= 6.3-.92=5.38

•Maximum profit/share= 15-5.38= 9.62

This gives us a reward risk of $1.78, which isn't all that great, to be honest. As you can see, the vagaries of option pricing affect the profit and loss calculations quite a bit. In this case, due to the existing sentiment on AAPL, perhaps the far month calls are priced lower than the near month.

Bear Put Spread

A bear put spread strategy can be used in a trade where you expect the value of the underlying asset to drop. In this case, you will make two transactions, buying at the money puts and selling out of the money puts. This creates a debit spread where there is an upfront cost. By making the buy and sell transactions simultaneously, you reduce the initial cost of the trade.

Using this strategy, you make a profit when the underlying asset decreases in price and also with the decrease in time value of the contracts. With a bear put spread, the potential for losses occurs when the underlying asset increases in value.

Pros:

- Reduced costs of entering a position
- Potential for a big return on investment

- Suitable for beginners
- Low and medium trading levels required

Cons:

- Your profit potential is limited

Credit Spread Options Strategy

This trading strategy involves buying and selling options based on the same underlying security. Both of these transactions should have the same expiration period though the strike prices will differ. The credit spread strategy is important because it serves as a tool for managing your risk exposure. It limits the potential risk of losses and, in this way, helps to prevent huge losses on your investment.

Depending on whether you expect the underlying asset to rise or fall, you can create a credit put spread or a credit call spread, respectively. In a credit put spread, you stand to gain a maximum profit limited to the premium you receive. For this to happen, the stock price should be higher than the strike price at the expiration of the options contract.

The other two of the four Vertical Spreads strategies are the Bear Call spreads and the Bull Put spread.

Bear Call Spreads

Bear or short call spreads are a trade that has an inverted reward risk profile but an extremely high success rate, assuming everything is executed well. This is a strategy that a lot of professionals love, thanks to it being a steady income earner. However, risk management is absolutely critical since the potential loss you could incur is many multiples of the amount of money you stand to make.

This is a strategy where money keeps flowing in with small wins but executes something wrong, and one loss will wipe everything away. A lot of beginners experience this due to getting complacent after the steady stream of money coming in.

This strategy is for sideways markets which are at a resistance zone or bearish markets. While selling a call is the best way to take advantage of a bear market, it is unlikely your broker will allow you to do this right off the bat. Hence, the bear call spread is an excellent strategy to deploy in such times.

How it Works

With a bear call spread, you will be writing an at-the-money or slightly out-of-the-money call and buying a well out of the money option. Thus, on entering the trade, you will receive the premium from the lower strike price call and pay the lesser premium of the higher strike price call.

This is also the amount of your maximum profit on the trade. If the underlying stock increases in price beyond the first call, you will need to exercise your higher strike price call to buy the shares to fulfill the lower call being exercised. Thus, it is vital that your strike prices are close together and not too far apart, or else your trade will be stuck in a no man's land.

All of this is better illustrated via an example. AAPL is currently trading at $173.30, and the closest at the money call is $175, priced at $4.75. Now, let's assume $175 is a major resistance and that the stock is certain to turn back downwards once it reaches here. We write a call at $175 and earn the $4.75 premium.

It is a good idea to buy calls that are two steps past the lower strike price level. At this point in time, the strike price that is two steps away is the $180 call, which can be bought for $2.84.

Cost of trade entry/maximum profit per share = Premium received from writing lower call - Premium paid to purchase higher call = 4.75 - 2.84= $1.91/ share.

Maximum loss = Strike price of higher call - strike price of the lower call - net premium received on trade entry = 180 - 175 - 1.91 = $3.09/ share.

As you can see, the reward risk is inverted with this strategy. Now, the best-case scenario for this trade is for both options to expire out of the money. In that case, you don't need to bother exercising either one of them.

The no man's land scenario is if the lower call moves into the money, but the higher call doesn't. In this case, you'll have to buy the shares yourself, physically, at whatever the market price is, and deliver the shares thanks to the lower call being exercised.

The worst-case scenario is price moving past the higher call, in which case you'll need to exercise it and deliver it. You'll obviously eat the entire loss in this case. This is why it is very important to make sure the price is in a strong bear trend or is near a strong resistance from which it will turn downwards.

Given the risk of this strategy, I personally recommend beginners stick to options that are in the current month, instead of trying to capture the time decay of near-month options. The additional time risk is too much, and most beginners will not be able to manage risk well enough to stomach such losses.

Bull Put Spread

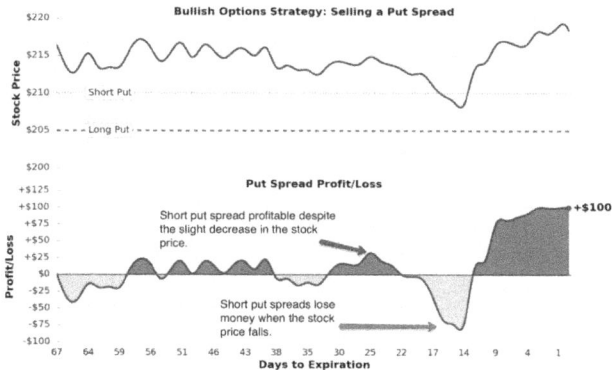

This strategy is used when you expect the underlying asset to rise in price but only by a small margin. It involves two transactions, selling, writing, puts, and buying puts. This strategy is a good alternative to the short put since it limits the potential for losses and therefore carries a lower risk.

In a bull put spread strategy, you should buy and sell puts that have the same date of expiration. In a bull put spread, the profit potential is determined by the difference between the price the strike prices of the contracts that you buy and the ones that you write. You gain more if the difference is significant, but you also stand to lose more in this scenario if the markets go against you.

Pros:

- You stand to gain even if the underlying asset does not increase in price
- Your potential losses are limited
- You can calculate both the maximum profit and loss potential from the onset

Cons:

- Your profits are limited

- Not ideal for beginners
- Requires medium or high trading level

CHAPTER 6: TOP OPTIONS TRADING STRATEGIES FOR BEGINNERS

The beauty of market-neutral strategies like the covered call and the collar is that they are conservative by nature and yet are powerful in terms of the returns they generate. You don't need to do anything fancy beyond learning a few technical-sounding names to impress others at cocktail parties!

A well-executed collar will pre-define your maximum gain and loss in advance. This way, you know exactly what will happen if the market behaves in a certain manner and can rest knowing that no matter what happens, your risk is defined fully and you need not worry about slippage or volatility.

Do note that there is the possibility of loss. The covered call does not have this component to it, but the collar does. Hence, the collar is the first strategy we'll deal with where defining your risk per trade becomes important. While I don't like putting a number of strategies, you can conservatively expect around 10-12% per year with the collar strategy.

This might sound like it's not worth it, given that a basic index fund has returned the same over the years. Well, consider that this is a market-neutral strategy, so you're insulated against up and down movements, unlike in an index fund. Second, index fund data is averaged over eighty years. Within those stretches, there have been decades where real returns have been negative.

There is a wide range of options trading strategies, but you do not need to utilize all of them. Identifying strategies that work for your particular trading plan is far more important than trying to employ dozens of strategies all at once. While the appropriate strategy will vary depending on factors such as market conditions, type of trade, and even budget, there are some strategies every trader at the beginning should be aware of. Let's go through the main three ones.

Covered Calls

The covered call is the perfect introductory trading strategy for beginners. It has a simple thesis that you can execute, and there's no need to adjust the trade in any way. While you don't need to adjust any options trading strategy listed in this book, the option is always available.

This adjustability often leads beginners to confuse themselves and complicate matters. None of this exists with the covered call. As a bonus, the covered call can be implemented simply as an extension of your regular investment activities in your retirement account.

Strategy

The underlying theory behind the covered call is the lowering of the cost basis of your stock purchase. For example, if you purchase 100 shares of AMZN for your retirement account or regular investing account, if you could lower the price you paid for the stock over time, you give yourself a lot more wiggle room with respect to how the market performs.

For example, if you purchased AMZN shares at $150 per share and the market declines to $145, you're carrying a $5 loss. Well, what if you could use a strategy that would make your purchase price effectively $140? In that case, you're still in a profit. The covered call is that strategy.

In fact, with a covered call, it is entirely possible to end up owning a stock for effectively zero cost.

Specifics

The strategy itself is quite simple. You need to write out of the money calls against your long stock holdings. Remember how I said that writing calls are a risky business and that brokers will not allow you to do this? Well, the covered call solves that problem because you're writing calls on a stock you already own. Therefore, the broker will not see this as a massive risk because in case the call's strike price is hit, you have stock to sell to the buyer. Hence the term 'covered.'

The time frame for this strategy is usually 30-45 days at the most. Ideally, you will write options for the far month. There is a very good reason to do this. You see, far month options usually have the highest amount of time value to them, even if they're not as liquid as the near month options. When an option enters thirty days before its expiry date, it begins to lose its time value massively.

The rate at which time value decays is almost exponential, with the decay being very less during the initial stages and rapid the closer it approaches expiry. Therefore, you'll receive the highest possible premium if you write a call sixty days out.

Now, there are some risks to this strategy. For one, your ideal situation would be to hold onto the stock and earn a good premium to reduce your valid purchase price. There is a line you need to walk here. On the one hand, writing a call that is far out-of-the-money will bring you a minimal premium. So, you want to write a call that is out-of-the-money but is plausibly close enough to warrant a decent premium.

However, the closer the strike price is, the greater your risk of the option moving into the money and being exercised. Here's the easiest way to approach this dilemma, and it doesn't involve any fancy technical market stuff. It has everything to do with your mental approach and risk management.

Do not think of the covered call as a strategy that makes you money (even though it does). Instead, think of it as you earning interest on your long position and compare it to an instrument that gives you a savings account in the stock market. When viewed this way, you'll eliminate the possibility of greed entering the equation since your expectations will be low.

Iron Condor

Why use an Iron Condor

Traders use iron condors because it's a limited risk strategy that can generate a regular trading income. Selling an iron condor is analogous to selling a put credit spread in that you are going to need a certain amount of collateral to cover the trade. So, while the iron condor is in your account, the money you use to protect it will be held until you close the position, or you let the options expire, assuming that you don't incur losses because the share price remains in the range that you've set up for the trade.

Let's consider a real-world example. The losses are not necessarily equal. In this example, we think of an iron condor on Facebook with strike prices of $192.50 and $212.50. It is quite a wide range; it's wide enough that it might survive the upcoming earnings call. Maximum losses occur when the share price goes above the high strike price call or below the low strike price put. In this example, the high strike price call is $215. The short strike price set is $187.50.

On the upside, if the share price rises above $215, there is a maximum loss of $55.

On the downside, if the share price goes below $187.50, the maximum loss is $305. The collateral required is always the larger of the two potential losses, so to enter into this trade, you'd have to deposit $305 into your account.

You can see that if the share price stays in between the inner strike prices, the maximum profit of $195 (the credit received for selling to open the position) is realized.

The assignment's risk is the same as for a put credit spread or calls credit spread, it's not something you have to worry about. Provided there's an assigned assignment that is all handled automatically by the broker, and the stocks will be quickly bought and sold without you even noticing.

So, the credit received on a per-share basis is $1.95. The upper put strike price gives the breakeven point on the downside minus the credit received, $192.50 - $1.95 = $190.55. The upper breakeven point is provided by the lower call strike price plus the credit received, so in this case, that would be $212.50 + $1.95 = $214.45.

For the strike prices, you choose out of the money values. An iron condor is considered a non-directional strategy. You only care that the share price stays within a given range of values, you don't care if it goes up or goes down within that range.

When to use an Iron Condor

You want to use an iron condor when there is no expectation for stock to move very much. Some people pick options with shallow delta values like 0.16, so they are far outside the money. It can give the store a more comprehensive range of values to oscillate around in, but you will make smaller profits per option contract. That said, it increases the probability of earning a profit. So, once again, we have a tradeoff.

You will not want to put an iron condor on when the stock has a high amount of implied volatility. High implied volatility will mean that there is a higher probability that the stock will move outside one of the boundaries that you have set up with the iron condor.

One situation that definitely would not go with an iron condor is before an earnings call. You do not want to have an iron condor in stock before the earnings call. If the stock rises to a new range, then it might be possible to use an iron condor to earn income off the store after it has settled down.

You might choose low volatility stocks for iron condors. For example, a relatively stable supply like IBM (outside of earnings season) could be a possible choice. But like any options trade, you will want to see what the open interest is on the options you are considering for your iron condor.

Bull Put Spread

We have already analyzed this strategy in the chapter "Vertical Spread Options Strategies." I just wanted to point out that this was a strategy recommended to anyone who is starting with options trading because I personally find it a very good strategy not to risk big losses. this, as you can understand, is very important at the beginning of the career of every trader, both from the financial point of view and moral.

CHAPTER 7: MORE BULLISH OPTIONS STRATEGIES

Married Put

In a married put methodology, a speculator buys (or at present claims) a specific resource (for example, shares) and at the same time buys a put option for a comparable number of shares. Financial specialists will utilize this technique when they are bullish on the benefit's cost and wish to ensure themselves against potential here and now misfortunes. This methodology basically works like a protection strategy and builds up a story should the benefit's value dive drastically. This is where an investor buys stock and equivalent put options simultaneously. You can sell the put option at the strike price. Just like the covered call, each married put contract requires 100 shares. In this case, the trader is positive that the stock value will rise, but uses a put option as insurance should the value go down.

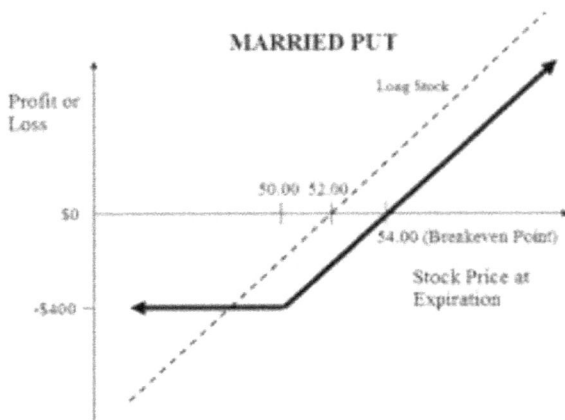

MARRIED PUT

The married put strategy is common in investors who have a vision of minimizing their stock's downside risk. When an investor buys the shares and an option, he protects his stock from loss should an adverse event occur and makes some cash as its value increases. However, if the stock does not go down, the investor loses the cash placed on the put option as a premium.

The married put has so many similarities with the covered call. It gets its name from combining or marrying a put option with the under-lying stock. For every 100 shares, you are only allowed to buy one put option.

The maximum profit for this strategy is undefined. The more the stock appreciates, the higher the profits. One downside of this strategy lies in the cost of premiums. The put option increases in value as the stock value declines, and because of this, the trader loses the cost placed on the option. However, such losses cannot be compared to the value of the underlying stock that would have been saved in the process.

Collars

We're taking the complexity up a notch with the collar. Collars involve a covered call, but there is an additional layer or leg to the trade, which is a protective put. Collars are more attractive than covered calls because, under certain circumstances, they can be completely risk-free and truly market neutral.

Implementing this strategy does require you to have a decent grasp of market environments such as ranges and trends.

CHAPTER 8: MORE BEARISH OPTIONS STRATEGIES

Covered put

Call options are a type of options contract that has a buyer whose outlook is bullish and a seller whose outlook is bearish. This means that the individual buying the option believes that the underlying asset is going to increase in value, and the seller believes that the underlying asset is going to decrease in value. Based on this nature, a call option buyer will earn a profit when the underlying asset experiences an increase in price value.

A covered put is a popular form of call option strategy that is made when the investor only expects a small increase or decrease in the cost of the underlying asset. These particular calls generate income through premiums, which are the prices that people pay in order to purchase the options.

The benefit of a covered put is that the investor gets into the option with the intention of holding a long position with the underlying asset. This way, they experience downside protection while also being able to generate passive income for the individual invested in this particular stock.

The big difference here is that a regular call option is taken for the short-term position, whereas a covered put option is taken for the long-term position. In the end, the covered put provides higher risk protection and greater earning potential.

CHAPTER 9: MORE NEUTRAL OPTIONS STRATEGIES

Strangle Options Strategy

This strategy is used in conditions where the market is volatile. It is ideal when you want to make a profit regardless of the direction in which the price of the underlying asset moves. When using the strangle options strategy, you hold a call and a put on the same underlying asset with different strike prices but a similar expiration period.

In a short strangle strategy where you sell both a put and a call that are out of the money, you make a profit from the premiums of the trade. This is why a short strangle is considered a credit spread. In a long strangle strategy where you buy both a put and call, this is considered a debit spread since you pay in order to open the position.

Ultimately strategies are the tools that every trader needs to make a return on their investment in different market conditions. Equipping yourself with knowledge on the different strategies, when, and how they are used will go a long way in ensuring you trade profitably.

Straddle Options Strategy

Using a straddle options strategy involves the buying and writing of an equal number of calls and puts. These transactions should have a similar strike price and expiration date. When you use this strategy, you create one position that will offset any loss to the other position in such a way that you still make a profit on the trade.

In markets with high volatility, you would use a long straddle. This is where you buy a put and a call with the same expiration period and strike price. The aim here is to profit regardless of which way the market moves. In markets with low volatility, a short straddle is more appropriate. Here, you collect a premium from writing a call and a put with a similar strike price and expiration periods.

Strategies for a Neutral Market

One advantage of trading options is that the price of an asset or security does not need to move significantly lower or higher than the strike price for you to make money. In neutral markets where the underlying asset does not undergo any significant upward or downward movement, neutral market strategies are used to enable the trader to make a profit.

When there is neither a decline nor a rise in the price of an underlying asset, the price is said to be moving sideways. In such circumstance, the strategies that you can use to get a return on your investment include:

Short Straddle

This strategy is used when you do not expect the price of the underlying asset to move much in either direction. When using this strategy, there are two transactions involved, write calls, and write puts. In this scenario, you will use a sell to open order to write at the money calls and also write puts on the particular underlying asset that you have chosen.

When you use the short straddle, you receive credit upfront since in both transactions you are writing options. This strategy is pretty straightforward and can be used when you want to profit from a neutral market. It combines short calls and short puts to enable you to make a profit from the effects of time decay on the contracts.

Pros:

- Upfront payment

Cons:

- Potential for heavy losses if the underlying asset moves significantly
- Requires high trade level

Short Strangle

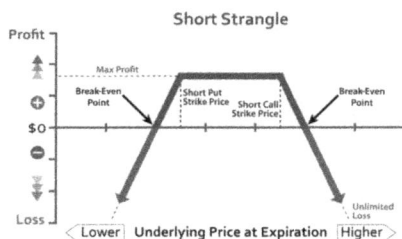

In a short strangle you, write call options on a particular underlying asset as well as an equal number of puts on the same asset. In this scenario, you will need to pick an appropriate expiration date bearing in mind that a short expiration increases your potential for success. Long-term expiration will be more risk but also have higher profit potential.

Pros:

- You receive an upfront payment

Cons:

- Requires a high trading level
- There is a high potential for losses

Strategies for a Volatile Market

When a market is unpredictable and prone to wide fluctuations, it is referred to as a volatile market. Volatile markets are risky to trade in, so it is not possible to predict which way prices will go. In such market conditions, there are some trading strategies that you can use to minimize your risk exposure.

Long Straddle

A long straddle is a volatile market strategy that carries limited risk. It is simple and straightforward, and even novice traders can use this strategy. A long straddle is used when you expect an underlying asset to move significantly, but you are not sure whether it will rise or fall.

This strategy uses a long call and long put, using at the money options contracts. In this scenario, you use the same expiration date for both transactions bearing in mind that a longer expiration increases your profit potential. Ideally, when using the long straddle strategy, you should purchase at the money options or those that are close to the current trading price of the underlying asset.

Pros:

- High-profit potential
- Simple and straight forward
- Low trading levels required

Cons:

- Potential for losses if the underlying security remains stagnant

Long Strangle

This strategy is used in volatile markets where you want to gain from a significant price move. When you use the long strangle, you stand to make a profit regardless of the direction in which the price of the underlying asset moves. Since it is a relatively low-risk and simple strategy, it is very popular in options trading.

To use the long strangle, you need to buy calls on the chosen asset and also purchase an equal number of puts on the same asset. These transactions should be made simultaneously on out-of-money options contracts.

Pros:

- Suitable for beginners
- Requires low trading levels
- Potential for unlimited profit
- Limited losses

Long Gut

This is an ideal options trading strategy in a volatile market where you cannot predict which direction the price of the security will move in. It involves two transactions, buying calls and buying puts. In this scenario, you purchase money call options and an equivalent amount of put options. These two transactions should be based on the same asset and have a similar expiration period.

Depending on whether you expect a quick or gradual movement in the price of the asset you can choose a short or long expiration date respectively. There is unlimited potential for profits when you use the long gut strategy if the underlying asset experiences a significant movement in price.

Pros:

- Simple strategy
- Low commission charges
- Low trading level required

Cons:

- High upfront cost

CHAPTER 10: MONEY AND RISK MANAGEMENT

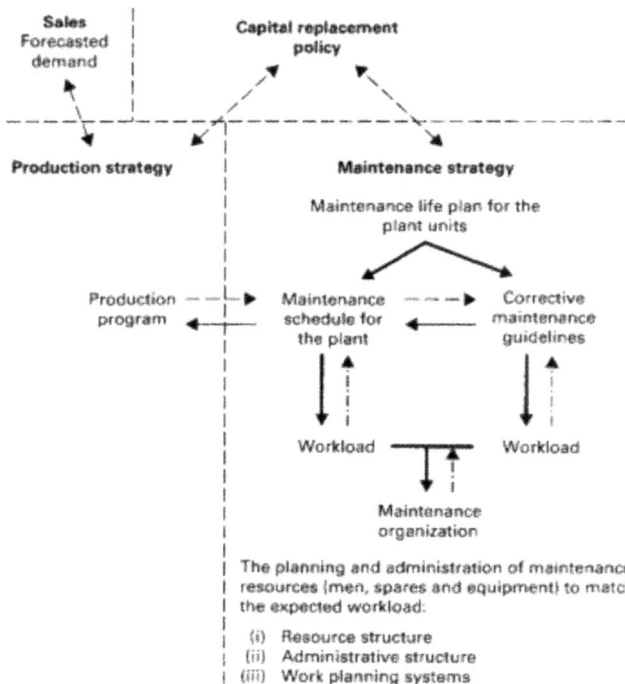

Money Management

Effectively dealing with your capital and risk exposure is basic when trading options. While risk is unavoidable with any type of invest-ment, your exposure to risk doesn't need to be an issue. The key is to deal with the risk funds viably; constantly ensure that you are alright with the level of risk being taken and that you are not exposing yourself to unreasonable losses.

Similar ideas can be applied while dealing with your money as well. You ought to be trading utilizing capital that you can afford to lose; abstain from overstretching yourself. As effective money and risk management are completely vital to fruitful options trading, it's a subject that you truly need to comprehend. We will take a look at a portion of the techniques you can, and should, use for controlling your budget and managing your risk exposure.

- Managing Risk with Options Spreads
- Managing Risk Using Options Orders
- Managing Risk through Diversification
- Using Your Trading Plan
- Money Management & Position Sizing
- Using Your Trading Plan

It's imperative to have a nitty-gritty trading plan that spreads out rules and parameters for your trading exercises. One of the pragmatic uses of such a plan is to assist you in dealing with your money and your risk exposure. Your plan ought to incorporate details of what level of risk you are OK with and the amount of capital you need to utilize.

By following your plan and just utilizing the money that you have explicitly distributed for options trading, you can keep away from probably the greatest mix-up that traders and investors make: utilizing "scared" money.

When emotion assumes control over, you possibly begin to lose your concentration and are obligated to behave irrationally. It might make you pursue losses from past trades turned sour, for instance, or making transactions that you wouldn't generally make. If you follow your plan and stick to utilizing your investment capital, then you should have a greatly improved potential for the success of monitoring your emotions.

Managing Risk Using Options Orders

A moderately basic way to manage risk is to use the scope of various orders that you can place. Also, the four fundamental order types that you use to open and close situations, there are some of the extra orders that you can place, and a considerable lot of these can help you with risk management.

For instance, a typical market order will be filled at the best accessible price at the hour of execution. This is a consummately typical approach to purchase and sell options; however, in a volatile market, your order may wind up getting filled at a value that is higher or lower than you need it to be. By utilizing limit orders, where you can set maximum and minimum prices at which your order can be filled, you can abstain from purchasing or selling at less ideal prices.

There are orders that you can utilize to motorize leaving a position: whether to lock a profit already made or cut losses on a trade that didn't turn out well.

By utilizing orders, for example, the cutoff stop order, the trailing stop order, or the market stop order, you can easily control what you leave a position.

This will assist you with avoiding situations where you miss out on profits by holding on to a position for a long time or incur large losses by not closing out on a terrible position rapidly enough. By utilizing options orders suitably, you can restrict the risk you are presented to on every single trade you make.

CHAPTER 11: TIPS TO TRADE LIKE A PRO

Know When to Go Off the Manuscript

While sticking to your plan, even when your emotions are telling you to ignore it, is the mark of a successful trader, this in no way means that you must blindly follow your plan 100% of the time. You will, without a doubt, find yourself in a situation from time to time where your plan is going to be rendered completely useless by something outside of your control. You need to be aware enough of your plan's weaknesses, as well as changing market conditions, to know when following your predetermined course of action is going to lead to failure instead of success. Knowing when the situation is changing versus when your emotions are trying to hold sway is something that will come with practice, but even being aware of the disparity is a huge step in the right direction.

Avoid Trades That Are Out of the Money

While there are a few strategies out there that make it a point of picking up options that are currently out of the money, you can rest assured that they are most certainly the exception, not the rule. Remember, the options market is not like the traditional stock market, which means that even if you are trading options based on underlying stocks buying low and selling high is just not a viable strategy. If a call has dropped out of the money, there is generally less than a 10% chance that it will return to acceptable levels before it expires, which means that if you purchase these types of options, what you are doing is little better than gambling, and you can find ways to gamble with odds in your favor of much higher than 10%.

Never Get Started Without a Clear Plan for Entry and Exit

More important than setting entry and exit points, however, is using them, even when there is still the appearance of money on the table. One of the biggest hurdles that new options traders need to get over is the idea that you need to wring every last cent out of every successful trade. The fact of the matter is that, as long as you have a profitable trading plan, then there will always be more profitable trades in the future, which means that instead of worrying about a small extra profit, you should be more concerned with protecting the profit that the trade has already netted you. While you may occasionally make some extra profit ignoring this advice, odds are you will lose far more than you gain as profits peak unexpectedly and begin dropping again before you can effectively pull the trigger.

Start with Enough Capital

One of the first things that you need to make sure that you are set with is enough capital to help you get into the investment. Capital is the amount of money that you can place into your account to help pay for any of the transactions that you choose, and that can be used if you end up experiencing a loss while you are trading.

You should always leave a little bit of money in your trading account. This is going to help you out when you are in the middle of a trade and can make it easier for your broker to keep working on trades without having to worry about a delay while your fund's transfer.

See the Positive About It and Find Opportunities

The following time you notice there is a situation with trading that has brought a lot of panic on, you should immediately take the opposing side. Some of the best trades you can make involve the trade having been cleared out from people panicking and using their market orders, without understanding that the doors for exiting are not as large as they believe or assume.

This doesn't mean all of the merchandise that people leave out of panic is worth investing in over long periods. Usually, when the market or stocks get socked, there will be a bounce-back that lets you leave in a better position than you would have if you went along with what everyone else was doing when they left too fast.

Trade at the Right Times

Since you are going to learn how to avoid big risks when you are an options trader, you are going to learn how to be very careful about your timing when it comes to entering and exiting the market. You have to be able to read the market the right way so that you can learn the best time to do both of those tasks. These investors have spent their time doing some research, and they know how to look at the big picture, rather than always calling up the broker and hoping that they can trust that person.

Learn How to Be Focused

There are quite a few people who have an idea that options trading is super easy, and then they jump in and become overwhelmed by what they are dealing with. If you are not used to this kind of investment, it may seem a bit hard to deal with in the beginning.

If you find that you are a person who is not able to easily focus on the task that you need to, then it is easy to have trouble with options trading because you are missing out on things. A trader who can maintain their focus for a long time is more likely to get more out of this trading style.

Never Follow the Crowd

One of the worst things that you can do is try to follow the crowd and hope that will work out well for you. Many beginners find it easy to look to the experts for advice, and then they will follow exactly what that expert says without doing any of their research or trusting their judgment. There is nothing wrong with getting advice from an expert, but your plan is not going to be the same as theirs. You are the only one who has an idea of your limits and your goals, and while you can listen to the advice that others give you, it is important to think for yourself and pick out a plan that works for you.

Keep It as Simple as Possible

Options trading is a complicated market by definition. You do not need to perplex things any further. Keep your strategies as simple as possible, use the simplest technical analysis tools, and manage your money in the simplest way possible. The rest will fall in place on their own.

Do Not Overtrade

When you start dealing with inexpensive options, it will be very easy to lose track of what you are trading with. Keep the number of contracts at a manageable level.

Pay Attention to Rankings

Especially if you are dealing with spreads, and particularly if you are a novice. Qualification rankings are available to consult at all times. An option that is not ranked high is not a good option, and it will probably cost you money.

Be Consistent

Before you ever make any trade, you are going to want to have a clear idea of the strengths and weaknesses of the various stocks in question as well as the best point to enter into a trade and at what point you are going to want to exit the trade if things go poorly, and also where you will exit if things ultimately go, as well as you could expect. Once you have made a plan, it is important to stick with it even if your emotions are making a compelling argument for going in another direction instead. It is important to always trust in your plan as it was made during a period when you were thinking as rationally as possible; giving in to your emotions at this point is akin to gambling with your investments.

Keep the Mood of the Market in Mind at All Times

Fundamental and technical analysis is all well and good, but they will only take you so far before you run into instances where the market seems to balk at the logical choice and move off in an unexpected direction. This typically happens when the will of the market goes against the status quo thanks to an unexpected outpouring of support from traders who are thinking with their guts instead of their brains. The best way to go about doing this is to keep tabs on what the major players in your market of choice are up to, as this will typically act as a litmus test when it comes to the feelings of the market as a whole.

Keep a Trading Journal

While it might seem to be a waste of time at first, the fact of the matter is that keeping a journal of all of the trades you make can be an extremely effective way to analyze what you are doing right, as well as what you are doing wrong when it comes to options trading. While one type of analysis or the other might pique your interest when it comes to trading at the moment, keeping a trading journal will allow you to look at your trading results from a more analytical perspective once you have gotten a little more distance and perspective on what it is that you are doing.

To get the most out of this process, you are going to want to keep track of each trade you make along with the date, the state of the market, and the underlying asset that you were basing all of your trades on, whether the trade ended up being profitable or not and your emotional and mental state while you were trading.

These tips should be enough to get you started. As time passes by, you will learn what options to look for and what to avoid. Remember that seasoned traders are considered those who have spent years on this business, not just a few months.

How to Keep Investing for the Long Term even during Bear Markets

We all know that market gives us approximately 10% in the long term. I do not care about your age. I care about how long you want to work. You could be in your 20's, 30's, 40's, 50's, or even 60's. If you have more than ten years to retire, then you should be building your portfolio and buying equities.

If you see that VIX is peeking... how will you know? I have this rule. If the VIX values are more than 70, then usually it's a bottom or a temporary bottom and is a good time to buy.

Another way to figure out is that the market has been falling for a few days; everyone is crying about the stock market. Everyone is worried. People on CNBC are all looking sad or at least not smiling!

Dalbar organization compared average mutual funds investors' returns with the index. Their main finding was that after the market goes up, investors put cash into the funds (buy high), and then after the market goes down, they take it out (sell low). They found that the average holding period for mutual funds was 2–4 years over the last 35 years, although mutual funds are supposed to be long-term investments. Because of this behavior, average investors underperform the indexes in both rising and falling markets. For example, in 2018, the average investor underperformed the S&P 500 by 5.04%.

CHAPTER 12: OPTIONS TRADER MINDSET

Being self-disciplined

I am sure after reading this book, you may be excited about the possibility of gaining financial freedom by using options trading. If you are willing to jump with both feet in, I applaud you. I also implore you to exercise caution and, therefore, self-discipline. Do not just stop your education on options with this book. Do more extensive research so that you can identify the best opportunities for you. Doing this will allow you to form the best strategy for your case and goals. Do not skip doing your homework because you are eager. Jumping the gun has led to many traders losing out. You need to rule your desires, wants, and actions rather than being ruled by them.

Being Committed

A successful options trader is one that does not give up. He or she does not trade on an on-again, off-again basis. This person is committed to the cause of building their financial success in this way and persists in their effort. Remember, I stated in the introduction of this book, that this is not a hobby. This is something you embrace as a business and part of your lifestyle. Go hard or go home. Options trading has no room for being tentative.

Continually Learning

The financial market is continuously evolving. It changes every single day. A successful trader needs to be able to roll with the punches and have a clear understanding of what is happening now. He or she needs to be able to make forecasts about the future as well. Continuously learning about the market also allows you to see new opportunities where amateur traders will not. One of the best ways to increase your knowledge of options is to follow the action of an experienced options trader. The point is not to copy his or her moves. Rather, it is to watch a master at work so that you can develop your own style of trading.

Being an Effective Risk Manager

There is no guarantee when you trade options, and as such, an effective options trader needs to be able to exploit his or her position to try to determine where he or she should take appropriate measures to capitalize on his or her gain. Part of managing risks involves being able to diversify your portfolio so that all your eggs are not in one basket. A successful trader does not go chasing after every available option. Neither does he or she get stuck chasing China eggs that do not yield gain. Even though there is no guarantee that it will all work out, being able to effectively manage risks significantly lowers the chances of the loss happening.

Being Able to Accept Losses Gracefully

The nature of the financial market is unpredictable, and every trader makes a loss at some point. Having an apt understanding of the market will minimize this loss, but you also need to be able to be flexible in how you handle this so that you do not get blindsided, nor do you let this weigh you down. Remember that any successful person needs to be able to find a lesson in their failure so that they come back stronger and better in the future.

CHAPTER 13: DAY TRADING OPTIONS

Day trading options have become more popular for several factors in recent years. The main reason is the possibility of a significantly higher return rate. Options give several additional benefits and would be an excellent way for day traders to achieve their financial objectives if used appropriately. You have got the right idea if you consider day trading options. You will learn in the following chapter about everything you need to know, which includes why you should start making daily trading options, how to exchange them, and tips.

Refreshing the Fundamentals

The Options are the type of contract which gives the holder, in general, just a few weeks or months, the privilege but not an obligation for purchasing or selling a stock or any other financial instruments around the given price.

For traders, different types of options are available and can be classified in many ways. Call options and put options are the two popular kinds of traders' options that all trades have been built from.

A stock call option allows the holder to purchase stock from the seller at a certain time at a certain price. When the price of the underpinning stock price increases, the value of the call option increases.

The holder is entitled to the stock option to be offered just before the expiry date for an agreed strike price. When the price of underlying stock price decreases, the value of an option decreases.

Why You Should Day Trade Options

Just that we have addressed the fundamentals, let us discuss why day stock options should be your trading market choice. You can make substantial money trading options for several reasons. Day trading with options is appealing even for several good reasons unless financial compensation is put to one side.

Facility to Trade

First, it's simple to trade options. It's like the purchase and sale of stocks. Users can pick from many purchasing options and then click on the purchase button.

Capacity to Hedge

Trading options offer a chance to work on either side of the market as both calls and put options can be purchased and sold. Therefore, if something bad happens on the short or the long side, you could even shield most of the capital.

Leverage

Second, the traders of options can get a very good payout with a little money because they can use the leverage options available.

Low Demand for Cash

People can most likely start with a reasonable amount of cash if they want to generate decent revenues as a day trader. But you can begin with far less cash if, kudos to leverage, you offer trading options rather than stocks. Options trading by the day provides you with such a quicker, less risky opportunity than most other securities, like mutual funds and stocks, to enter and leave positions. It is also much cheaper to buy an option than to purchase the underlying asset, such as stock shares. So, with much less capital, you could even control the same number of shares.

Diversity

As options are much cheaper than that of the actual stock purchase, you can take advantage of increased investments. The capital will go even further, and profit potential is increased.

Greater benefits

You could even benefit from an option when a stock moves. Let's say that stocks move from 25 dollars to 50 dollars. That would lead to a 100% share gain. Nevertheless, a call option would bring you a 500 % gain from $1 for every contract to $5. Users can therefore gain more and less from an option in less time.

Options may be successful if other businesses fail – options can achieve success while some market sectors fail, partly because you don't have to make use of your option. Furthermore, it can benefit from volatility itself.

Mutual incentives - Although stock-based options often are combined, they could bring more advantages. You could indeed sell the option to generate revenue on the inventories you already have.

The trading with intraday options is multiple and has great profit potential. However, accessibility is the smartest idea. Trading options from everywhere in the world can start in a day. An internet connection is all you need.

How a day trader can Day Trade Options?

Once, the domain of the Wall Street elite was regarded as options trading. The proliferation of online brokerages means that everybody needs to get a little starter fund and also a little bit of know-how of the options that are being traded currently.

People need to know a few basic tools for daily trader choices:

A Computer or a Laptop

It is desirable, but not necessary, to have two monitors in the first place. The computer needs a fast processor and must have enough memory to prevent crashes or delays when running the trading programs.

A Broker Online

You should find an online broker offering trading options such as TD Ameritrade and TradeStation or trading options.

A Fast, Reliable Internet Connection

Options Day Traders should use an internet connection of at least cable type or an ADSL. While speeds are different for these kinds of services, an intermediate Internet package is essential.

How Day Trading Works?

Day traders work in a compressed window of time. Let's assume that a day trader buys 500 shares of a stock at 9 am. After half an hour, the price for the stock begins to rise and the day trader sells the stock. If the stock has a rise in price by $0.50 per share, the day trader will bag $250 minus commission.

Some day traders use the scalping technique which aims at making small profits by following little price changes throughout the day. Range trading is also popular among day traders as it employs support and resistance techniques to determine decisions about buying and selling. As already mentioned, there is the third technique known as news-based trading. Traders benefit from the volatility that originates due to different pieces of news. Another technique is known as high-frequency trading (HFT) in which a trader uses algorithms to exploit inefficiencies in the markets.

There is a big difference between swing trade and day trade. The difference hails from their definitions, it goes a mile ahead to time spent in and risks involved in both forms of trade. Day trade has lower risk involvement, but one has to spend more of his or her time, unlike swing trade. Day traders are prone to participating in two forms of trade which are long trades or short trades. Long trade involves an individual purchasing the financial instruments and selling them after them increasing in value. On the other hand, short trade involves selling financial instruments and later purchasing them after their prices have dropped.

The trading market has undergone several advancements. The major change was witnessed during the deregulation process. There was the creation of electronic financial markets during this period. One of the major innovations was the high-frequency trading index. It uses heavy algorithms to enable huge financial firms in stock trading to perform numerous orders in seconds. It is advantageous because it can also predict market trends.

What Benefits Do Day Traders Offer to the Market?

In terms of economic benefits, how does day trading benefit stock trading as a whole? Well, if anything, day traders provide liquidity to the stock market. They offer a ready base of buyers and sellers of the stock. This provides the necessary movement of a stock's price that may encourage other traders to look at either the short-term or long-term value or prospects of the stock. In other words, by providing action on a strictly short-term basis, day traders tend to shine a light on the overall attractiveness of a stock.

Keep in mind this is quite ironic because day traders, as a rule, do not look at the fundamentals of a stock. They don't look at the price/ earnings ratio or P/E. They don't look at long-term value, they don't look at industry positioning. They couldn't care less about any of that. Instead, they focus more on momentum, share movement, share volume and price velocity going either up or down.

Day trading Options with a Strategy

It is very important to learn some points before going towards the options market for day trading. They are:

Awareness is your Strength

Besides knowing basic trading practices, daily traders must keep up to abreast with the current stock market issues and updates affecting the stock such as the Federal Reserve's interest rate plans, economic prospects, etc.

Do the homework. Start making a checklist of stocks that you want to trade and also be aware of selected firms and overall markets. Search business news as well as visit trustworthy financial sites.

Set the Funds Aside

Evaluate the amount of capital that is prepared to risk for every trade. Numerous successful day traders risk somewhere around 1 to 2 % per trade. If you have a trade account with $40,000, you are to risk 0.5% of the trade capital, the maximum trade losses will be $200 (0.5% of $40,000).

Deposit an excess amount of money with that you can trade then you will lose. This could or could not happen, remember.

Set Aside some Time

It takes your time for day trading. That's why day trading is termed. Actually, you will have to give up most of the day. If your time is limited to set aside, then don't consider day trading options.

The approach involves a trader that can arise mostly during hours of trading, to monitor the markets and to spot opportunities. It's key to move fast.

Opening Small

As a beginner, during a session, focus on a maximum of 1 to 2 stocks. With only a few stocks, it is easier to track and find opportunities. It is increasingly prevalent lately that fractional shares can be traded so the specific, smaller amounts that you wish to invest can be specified.

This means that even if a person buys Apple shares for $250, numerous brokers also will let you purchase a 5th of the share but only wish to purchase $50.

Avoid Bribes

You probably would like to have deals and low prices but stay away from stocks of a penny. These stocks are usually illiquid and there are often bleak possibilities with hitting a jackpot.

Numerous stocks trading less than 5 dollars per share are de-listed from key exchanges and thus only traded over the counter (OTC). Be clear of these until you see a real chance while doing your research.

Time of Trades

As shortly as markets open in the morning, numerous orders placed by the investors begin to execute, which contributes to price volatility. The seasoned trader can identify trends and identify profits properly. Although it may be best for newbies to learn the market for 15-20 minutes without taking any steps.

Usually, middle hours are far less volatile and afterward move up to the clock again. Although rush hours provide opportunities, starting with it is safer for beginners.

Limit Order Cut Losses

Decide which kind of orders you are going to be used to enter and exit the trade. Are you going to be using market orders or limits? It is performed at the best price present at the moment, and therefore there is no price guarantee. If those who place the market order, the price, but not the execution, is guaranteed by a limited order. The Limit orders help trade more accurately and set prices for both buying and selling – not seem unrealistic but executable. Extra sophisticated experienced day traders can use options to protect their positions.

Be Realistic

Towards being profitable, a strategy does not have to win all of the time. Many traders succeed only 50 % to 60 % of their trade. Enter and exit techniques were often clearly defined as well as written down so that the risk for each trade is restricted to a certain proportion of the account.

Sometimes your nerves are tested on stock markets. You have to learn, as a day trader, to disregard greed, fear and hope. Decisions must be governed not through emotion, but by logic.

Keep to the Strategy

Successful traders must move quickly, but don't think quickly. What is the reason? Because they have established a trading strategy ahead of time and have adhered to the discipline. Instead of trying to make profits, obey your formula closely. Never let the emotions get one's best and give up on your strategy.

Beginners Mistake to Avoid when you Choose to Day Trade the Options

Lack of a Plan

While trading, it is important that you have a plan. A plan acts as a compass direction while trading; it shows you the move that you should take to ensure that it is a wise trade decision. In a plan, we have different goals while trading. Some of these goals make our investment in day trading worth our while. They give us hope to achieve more out of life and, at the same time, inspire us to push beyond our abilities. A person's failure to create a plan fails. You find that you make investments without properly evaluating all the under-lying factors. In case there are some risks involved, you find that you are not aware of them. In turn, these risks exposed you to the possibility of encountering a loss. When such incidences occur, you are not well-prepared with risk management strategies since you failed to plan. A plan will help you achieve a lot in the trading industry. Most of the time, it provides a bearing for the direction that one is taking while trading.

Trading to Cover up for Previous Losses

Most traders are victims of this strategy. After conducting your daily trades, things may not move as planned. You find that you might have expected to get a profit out of the trades made, but instead, you end up with a loss. To cover up for the losses, you decide to engage in another trade, hoping that things will be different. Contrary to your expectations, you end up encountering more losses than you would have imagined. You get to a situation where you are full of regrets due to the wrong decision that you made. It is important to note that rushed decisions barely lead to anything good.

In most cases, they end up in sabotage, and you may not be able to recover from some of these incidences. We ought to learn that two wrongs do not make a right. Once you have made a mistake, the first step does not involve bouncing back to the same thing that caused you to make a mistake. You need to calm down and identify where you went wrong and start reorganizing from that point.

Overtrading

As a beginner, you may have started trading with huge expectations. You have this big dream of becoming an overnight success. You decide to invest heavily in your trades, especially after hearing what other traders are earning out of trading. Ideally, it is healthy to have self-belief and imagine that you, too, can get to the point that other investors have reached. While at it, you must have practical dreams that are achievable. Some people have managed to sell out the idea that trading is an easy task that can result in earning within minutes. However, many people start trading and end up with huge frustrations when they fail to achieve their dreams as fast as experts. You find that with the excitement of engaging in trading, you end up engaging in multiple trades to earn quick money. In this instance, most trade executions are not carefully planned; they are randomly selected. This means that you do not take time to develop the right strategies to succeed in the different trades, and eventually, you end up losing.

At the same time, we have individuals who spread their risks across different trades. You are uncertain if you will end up making a loss or a profit. In this instance, you decide to spread your risks so that regardless of how the trade goes, you will not experience a total loss. In the beginning, this looks like an attractive strategy, and it almost feels like it is impossible to make a complete loss. However, you should remember that you are taking a gamble. This means that you can either earn a loss or a profit in both situations.

The Belief That a Big Investment Leads to Profits

Some people tend to have a misplaced belief that they need to make a big investment to earn a profit. This belief has caused a lot of individuals to make numerous mistakes while trading. We have had people invest a huge amount of their earnings, only to end up making a huge loss. For instance, you have $100 in your account, and you end up investing $90. With such an investment decision, you cannot afford to make a loss. Any wrong move can result in sabotage and make you lose what you worked so hard to get. At this point, with such an amount, you may end up feeling depressed after you have made a loss. Remaining with $10 can be challenging, especially considering that you had more, yet you lost it from making a trading mistake.

At this point, we must learn to avoid placing all our eggs on one basket. In case of an accident, we may lose all the eggs and have none that is spared.

CHAPTER 14: SWING TRADING OPTIONS

How to Swing Trading Options

Swing traders face a gamble that no businessman wants to bear or to stay overnight. Keeping options overnight subjects, you to larger market movements, particularly if you may not have access to the pre- and post-market exchanging.

Options are mostly owned by long-term traders to offset company shares during turbulent times, but optional swing traders typically have one task to do: outsize gains. Option agreements are inexpensive, and profits can be significantly higher than the associated securities.

Swing options trading helps you to gain the benefit of short-term share swings, irrespective of depth or reach. A specific stock experiencing a relatively mild bout of turbulence could still witness the price of its options rising.

It is not uncommon for unconventional options to double or triple simultaneously during most exposed trading sessions. In fact, swing trading options will help to keep regular profit targets in line whenever the market trades weaker than IHOP pancake.

Options agreements can be bought for only some pennies based on how far you can get from actual asset values, but you have to purchase at least 110 contracts and buy in multiples of 110.

The closest you move to that "money" (actual current share value), the costlier the options would be. Many traders now give commission-free investment options, but still, cost a fee for each contract.

Options traders also have to live by standard day trading laws for accounts priced at less than $26,000. Pattern day trading rules are applied by brokers and will not permit you to exchange more than four days in the five-day period unless capital standards are met.

Although, if you are going for swing trading, you are going to deny this principle by keeping positions overnight. The Swing traders also have to think about Good Faith breaches if they purchase and sell unsettled funds.

Select a Side

Calls and placements are the two forms of options agreements. Purchasing a call option offers an investor the opportunity to 'call' shares if the actual security hits a specific pre-set value.

The put option seems to be the absolute opposite, buying a put enables an investor to 'put' shares on a counterparty (normally their broker) if the actual security comes at that predetermined price.

You may also compose options for the other traders to purchase, but these approaches are typically utilized to hedge assets. Writing options will open up theoretically infinite losses while purchasing options will restrict risks to premium instead.

If you believe any stock is about to fall in the short run, you'd look to purchase the put option that really is out of money (OTM). The OTM option, either a put or the call, indicates that the strike rate of the actual asset is still to be achieved.

If you purchase a 30 BAC put when the securities are trying to trade at $35, your put is assumed out of money.

Similarly, the 40 BAC call option seems to be out of money while securities are traded at $35. Thus, in the money (ITM) options could be utilized in specific complicated hedging approaches, but the swing traders typically focus on OTM agreements.

As regards the pricing of options contracts, it's basically just about assessing the likelihood of possible market occurrences. The more probable it is when anything occurs, the costlier an option will be, the more benefits from the case. For example, when the valuation of the underlying stock decreases, a call valuation goes up. The key is to knowing options relative value.

The less period an alternative has before expiry, the little interest it would have. That is because, when we get near to expiry, the price odds change in the underlying stock decrease. Of that purpose, wasted possession is an option. If you purchase an option of one month that's outside the bank, and the market does not change, with passing each day, the option is less attractive. Given that duration is an aspect of an option's quality, an option of one month would be less attractive than an option of three months. This is due to the price move probability in favor of you increases with the availability of more time and contrariwise.

Volatility also makes an option more expensive. Due to this, uncertainty pushes higher odds of a result. When the value of the underlying commodity decreases, the chances of major movements, up & down, rise with greater market fluctuations. Trading of options and uncertainty are, therefore, closely related to one another.

Swing Trading Strategies

To see success with swing trading, you need to make sure that you are working on the right strategy. There are a lot of different strategies that you can work with when you are ready to join the market, and each of them has the potential to earn you a profit if you properly use them. But you have to know how each of them will work, and you need to stick with that strategy throughout your whole-time trading.

Looking at Good Patterns

One thing that you can look at is the charts for a particular stock you would like to look through. There are a lot of different patterns that can come up all the time, and the way that they look will determine whether they are a good one to use for your trade or if you should go with another option. When you notice these patterns, you will be better able to predict how the stocks that you want to work with will behave in the future and use this to make a profit.

Ditch the Micro Time Frames

With swing trading, you must focus more on the longer time frames because they're less volatile, and by doing so, you minimize your risks for "false triggers" or whiplashes that can make you take positions on securities whose prices are still on a decline. The shortest time frame you should consider is daily, nothing less. The longer your time frame, the lesser the false triggers and noise you'll encounter, and the more you can maintain your winning swing trading streak.

Trend Following

No matter what strategy you decide to use, you will need to make sure that you understand how to read charts and trend lines.

Even though the current price is the most important price, you will want to pay attention to all of the prices that you see for every day that you take into your analysis.

Managing Your Money

One of the biggest tips to help you figure out how much money to put towards a stock is by evaluating the risks associated with the stock. You will be able to do this through any strategy that you will use and various other factors that are part of your trading plan.

Follow the Rules and Guidelines

One of the biggest reasons you need to make sure that you are following your guidelines is because the more consistent you are with your trading, the more likely you are to become successful. Furthermore, you will want to make sure that you follow the guidelines as they will help you to think systematically when it comes to making decisions.

Diversity

Diversity is one of the more popular controversies when it comes to trading. While some traders feel you need to have great diversity, which is a variety of stocks, in your portfolio, others feel that this isn't as important. In reality, the more serious you want to be with your trading, the more you will focus on diversity. However, this isn't always true when it comes to investors. But, as stated before, investing and trading are two different career paths in the stock market.

Pay Attention to the Float

However, this is also the trick when it comes to the float strategy. There tends to be a fine line between having a massive float and having a float that will give you the best profits. The reason why a massive float, which would be too many shares, can cause you to lose capital instead of increasing your profits is that if you have a huge float, the price won't move as quickly. However, if you have a smaller number of shares in your float, then you will find that the price moves a bit higher, of course, this gives you a larger profit. With this said, you also don't want to have too few shares in your float. If this happens, then you won't be able to make much of a profit either, as this can stop your float from increasing in price.

Breakout and Breakdown Strategies

When you focus on the breakout strategy, you are looking at the history of your stock's trend line in a microscopic fashion. When you are looking at the trend line, you will see every time the price has gone up and down. Stock prices are almost constantly changing throughout the day, which is what the trend line shows. Every now and then, you will notice in the trend line that you have several high points and several low points. These high points indicated the highest prices of the stock, and the lowest points show the lowest prices.

The biggest difference between the breakout strategy compared to the breakdown strategy is the condition of the market. If you notice that the stock has been going on an upward trend for a while, you will use the breakout strategy. However, if you notice that the trend shows the price has been decreasing over time, you will use the breakdown strategy.

News Playing

As you know by now, one of the most important parts of your day is your pre-trading portion. This is one of the first things you will do once you start your day. You will want to do this before you start trading; however, you will probably be checking out the stock market so you can see the changes in your stocks and any target stocks that you are watching.

However, one of the most important parts of this part of the day is reading the news that happened overnight. This is important because you need to know what news is going to affect what stock, especially if you own the stock. You should always make note that any type of news can affect the pricing of financial instruments. For example, if you read that a company donated a large amount of money towards a nonprofit organization, people might be more likely to invest in that stock. However, if you read any negative news about a company, you will find the stock price going down because people are selling their shares.

Be Flexible

While you want to follow the rules and guidelines, you should also remain flexible. First, you want to remember that life happens. Sometimes we plan to sit down to work but we have to go pick up a sick child from school or have a family emergency. When this happens, we might not be able to complete the financial instruments that we took on. This means that you will either keep them in your portfolio and take any loss or hope for some gain or you can trade them and close out for the day. When you are flexible, you will realize that this situation will be fine, and you won't dwell on the fact that you couldn't complete the job as you should have.

Remaining flexible will also help when you find yourself with unrealistic expectations, which is a common mistake among traders. On top of this, it will help you realize that mistakes happen and you shouldn't put too much emphasis on them.

Join an Online Community

Another great way to learn about swing trading and meet other traders is to join an online community. There are several websites that are comprised of forums run by some of the most experienced swing traders today. These forums are extremely beneficial to any trader for a variety of reasons. First, beginners can go join the community and receive more tips, trading lessons, and other information that will help them become successful. Second, this is often a location where beginners meet their trading mentor. Third, this is a place where traders can go to not only get the most up-to-date information on the profession but also get to know people who are like them. It is always important to feel that you are not alone, especially when you find yourself struggling with a part of trading. There will be hundreds, if not thousands, of people who will be interested in helping you.

Pick a Strategy that is Easy

Some beginners think that complex strategies are the best to increase their profits. But these complex strategies can be really confusing and overwhelming for someone who is just beginning. Go with a simple strategy, at least until you learn more about the market.

Look at Market Indicators

These market indicators can help you to determine which way your trading will go and are not things that you should avoid looking through.

Tips and Tricks from Swing Trading Experts

If you already have some experience trading in the foreign exchange market, you should also repeat the basic theory, because its understanding is built on deeper topics. In this chapter, you will get Forex tips, and these tips from swing trading experts I have researched to make your trading more profitable.

Choose a Licensed Broker

This is perhaps the most important point. Carefully choose a broker who will execute your orders. Take this process seriously. Look at the reviews of other traders, read the recommendations, check for licenses, because the broker must be reliable. There are many fraud brokers on the market, so in order not to fall for their bait, take enough time to check their reputation. One of the most reliable brokers in the foreign exchange market is Admiral Markets. You can open an account with this broker here.

Have a Strategy

When you decide which broker you want to work with, you will need to find a suitable strategy, or create one yourself. To do this, you first have to fully comprehend what your objectives are and how much money and effort you are prepared to invest in trade. In any case, in order to comprehend which method is most appropriate for you, first, you will have to attempt it in practice. This is usually accomplished by trading on a demo account. This way, you can shield yourself against having to lose actual cash.

Less means More

Among the most useful advice is starting small, no need to spend large amounts of money, especially for beginners. Even small investments could bring great returns for you. I, therefore, suggest that you invest a minimal quantity and boost your trade balance because of earned revenue. Besides, follow the 2 % rule—don't spend more than 2% of your stake in one deal. So, you lessen risks and learn how to get a stable income.

Avoid Stress

Perhaps this advice seems silly to you. But take it seriously. Trade so that you are calm. Experiences only conflict with trading. If you ponder the decision made, do not put it into usage. Or you can dig a little more extensive, find a few reasons to know that this decision was perfect, and then it's easy to execute it. Thus, you can safely trade while keeping a sober mind.

The Trends are Good

Some radical traders go against the pattern. As a principle, they're not lurking long on the foreign exchange market. Trends should always be used, particularly if you consider the long-term foreign-exchange investment. Trend trading allows you to comprehend what the market will offer you, and also helps to boost profits from currency trading while lowering the impact of risk in trading.

Study and Analyze

On the way to successful trading, you will have to work hard. You will need to learn how to quickly monitor markets, exchange rates, and track the trend. This usually takes a lot of time. But you will certainly pay off. Study and analyze the market to get even more income.

Find a Decent Broker

The success of trading depends on the choice of a broker by 50%. Many beginners ignore this advice, which they later regret. If you can find a good broker, stay with him. Take the time to look for a decent broker. Scroll through the forums, find the opinions of different traders to understand how things really are. A good broker should share your values and provide the highest quality services. And only after that, you can look at the terms of trade that he offers. Subscribing to a reliable broker will contribute to the success of your trading. If you have not decided on a broker yet, I advise you to consider the following option: Admiral Markets offers traders favorable conditions, and some of the lowest spreads in the foreign exchange market. In addition, they provide a large number of educational resources with which traders can engage in their self-education.

Plan for the Future

Experienced traders in currency are often urged to formulate a schedule.

Do you have to get from it what you want to achieve in a particular timeframe of time? In the pursuit of money, traders often forget why they came to trade at all. Never forget about previously outlined plans. Excitement turns traders to the head, and they go off the previously chosen path, subsequently getting lost in the vastness of the foreign exchange market. Before you open a deal, you should carefully analyze everything that can affect it. So, you can protect yourself from disappointment, well, and save your capital.

Keep an Eye on the Charts

Each market has its own graph and its analytical processes. When you plan on investing in several markets, you need to know how to interpret the details these charts provide. These are Forex tips that will help you to properly distribute your time and correctly organize your trading. Practice and immerse yourself in this until it is clear. Only thus will you make the most of those advantages given by the schedule.

Don't be Greedy

I understand that traders come to the foreign exchange market, mainly for money. But still, if you strive only to where potential income is potentially visible, you are unlikely to be able to earn anything. In Forex trading, greed prevents you from thinking soberly, that is, negatively affects the decisions you make. I understand that sometimes it's difficult to resist a tempting deal, but you must go within the framework of your trading plan. This item in the list of Forex tips and tricks will help you competently manage your money.

Always Try to Analyze Past Trades

If you take this statement seriously and develop an effective mastery in yourself, you will be able to comprehend the justification for your previous failures, reach conclusions and, therefore, not reiterate such a blunder any longer. I find this to be one of the most significant beginners' Forex tips.

Experiment

You always need to try and improve as you would in any company. In this, the consistent revelation of doing something innovative and unique will help, new tools, strategies, or schemes. This concludes this list of the top 20 Forex currency trading tips. Put your knowledge into practice and increase your profit.

Common Mistakes to Avoid in Swing Trading

Watching the Industry too Actively, too Often

Seeing a screen, waiting for each tiny campaign all day long could be harmful to both your psychological and financial health. You may wind up making numerous little trades from impulse as well as anxiety. That is the very last thing you wish to do when you are swing trading. As a swing trader, you should provide the stocks with enough space to breathe. This brings us to the subsequent point

Making Numerous Small Moves without Lots of Thought

Novice traders tend to need to trade every little step without looking at the larger picture. A decent trader does not open a trade in a sensitive position. They just wish to open a location once the odds are stacked in their favor. This can improve overall profitability. They only trade whenever there is a clear trend. In case there is none, they simply remain on the sidelines.

Getting Sidetracked by a Stock's Fundamentals

Swing traders make choices based on the cost at any moment. The price tag is the thing that pays you the profits. Do not make reactionary trades only due to an event concerning the stock's fundamentals. A stock's basics are just a distraction in swing trading strategy. Some swing traders make rash choices, and so they spend the price tag (literally). Always remember: When swing trading, the focus of ours is not in the end.

Lacking Discipline and Patience

Essential, boring, and unsexy as it may sound, persistence, as well as a subject, will be the crucial components to becoming a booming swing trader. What separates a beginner swing trader from a lucrative swing trader is withstanding the desire to make rash decisions. Typical errors noted are lacking persistence as well as discipline. Nevertheless, concentrating on the incorrect facets of swing trading could get us into difficulty, however.

Focus on Profits While not Managing Risk

This may seem to counter-intuitive, but swing trading is about dealing with risk, not concentrating on benefits. Without proper risk management, greed is going to get the best of any trader. Focus on turning into an excellent swing trader, and the earnings will come naturally. It is a clear point that many traders overlook when they are blinded by the eagerness to generate money. Manage your risk properly, cut losses, and minimize losing trades.

Attempting to Search for a Holy Grail

Finally, yet importantly, the majority of traders purchase stock trading programs wanting to locate the Holy Grail of nearly a hundred % accuracy in predicting trades. The cold fact is that the Holy Grail Product is an established method that works with your temperament and your objectives. There is not an infallible system. If there was, the marketplace would have disappeared, as a particular product will have mopped everything up. Losses are a component of trading. We have to confront them squarely and not be crippled by them.

Swing trading is a type of investing where you attempt to exploit the organic oscillations of stocks. Frequently stock prices move inside a specific range of prices with a given period, enabling you to take advantage of these periodic ups & downs. Swing trades are typically held for a couple of days to a couple of weeks, so it is much easier compared to day trading but does not require you to overlook the money you invested for a long time.

CONCLUSION

The best thing to do to get started is to buy some calls and puts on index funds. Start small, let your account grow, and accept that you will have some losses along the way. That is the reality when you decide to work with this type of investment or business—there is a risk for losses along the way. But that does not mean that losses will be a constant thing. If you play your cards right, really study the market, and make sound decisions, you are bound to rebound from your losses and start gaining profits. Risk is in everything that we do, and it all just varies depending on how we mitigate these risks and make them work to our advantage. We cannot predict how the market will fare daily, stock prices are affected by a lot of factors, and most of them are things we cannot control, that is one of the things that you need to keep in mind.

Patience and dedication are crucial when it comes to trading, especially options. You will be set up to be financially independent, to work at your own will, and as per your own schedule. You will not have to stay at one place to earn money. Knowing that all you need is an internet connection to work for a couple of hours and set up your next trading strategies, you can earn money while you are on the go.

If there is something we want you to know without a doubt after reading this book is that through Options Trading, you can reach your financial freedom and that there is no limit to the gains you can make if you have the correct information and if you are ready to do what it takes to be a successful trader.

The key to success is to simply never give up and to be resilient. Reduce the stress on yourself, and you'll be fine. Here's wishing you all the success in your options trading journey!

www.ingramcontent.com/pod-product-compliance
Lightning Source LLC
Chambersburg PA
CBHW071503210326
41597CB00018B/2674